Americans All biographies are inspiring life stories about people of all races, creeds, and nationalities who have uniquely contributed to the American way of life. Highlights from each person's story develop his contributions in his special field — whether they be in the arts, industry, human rights, education, science and medicine, or sports.

Specific abilities, character, and accomplishments are emphasized. Often despite great odds, these famous people have attained success in their fields through the good use of ability, determination, and hard work. These fast-moving stories of real people will show the way to better understanding of the ingredients necessary for personal success.

Mahalia Jackson

QUEEN OF GOSPEL SONG

by Jean Gay Cornell

illustrated by Victor Mays

GARRARD PUBLISHING COMPANY
CHAMPAIGN, ILLINOIS

For my mother, Florence Dixon Gay

Picture credits:

Columbia Records: pp. 58, 63
Globe Photos: pp. 66 (both), 70
Declan Haun, Black Star: p. 2
Constantine Manos, Magnum: p. 92
United Press International: p. 84
Wide World Photos: p. 75

Acknowledgment:

"We Shall Overcome"
Words and Music arrangement by Zilphia Horton,
Frank Hamilton, Guy Carawan, and Pete Seeger
TRO—© Copyright 1960 and 1963 Ludlow Music, Inc.,
New York, New York.   Used by permission.
Royalties derived from this composition are being
contributed to The Freedom Movement under the
trusteeship of the writers.

Library of Congress Cataloging in Publication Data

Cornell, Jean Gay.
    Mahalia Jackson: queen of gospel song.

    (Americans all)
    SUMMARY: A biography of the renowned gospel singer
who wanted more than anything else to "sing for the
Lord."

        1. Jackson, Mahalia, 1911–1972—Juvenile literature.
[1. Jackson, Mahalia, 1911–1972. 2. Singers, American.
3. Negro musicians] I. Mays, Victor, 1927–
II. Title.
ML3930.J2C67   783.7 [92] ₿ 73–14713
ISBN 0-8116-4581-9
                                                J

                                              C2

Contents

1. "Don't Tell Aunt Duke!"

Mahalia put her school books on the kitchen table and hurried into the living room. She wound up the record player and gently set the needle in place. The rich sounds of Bessie Smith's voice filled the room. The song was "St. Louis Blues," and Mahalia knew the words by heart. Trying to make her voice sound just like Bessie's, she sang along with the record.

The back door slammed, and Mahalia spun around to snatch the needle off the record. "Who's there?" she called quickly.

"It's only me," her brother Peter answered as he came in from the kitchen. "Don't worry, Aunt Duke won't be home for a while. But, Haley, she'll skin you alive if she catches you playing Cousin Fred's jazz records!"

"You wouldn't tell her, would you, Peter?"

"Of course not," he said, "but you know she thinks jazz is sinful. You sounded good, though—almost as good as Bessie Smith."

"Do you really think so, Peter, or are you just saying that?" Haley asked with a pleased smile.

"Well, at least you can sing as *loud* as she does," teased Peter.

"Oh, you!" Haley giggled. She knew she had a big, strong voice for a ten-year-old. When she sang in the Sunday school choir, she could be heard above all the others. Mahalia loved church music, but she liked jazz too.

New Orleans, where she was born on October 26, 1911, was a center for jazz musicians. Brass bands traveled in horse-drawn wagons and blared out their music all over the city. The wagons carried signs telling about picnics or dances or other events. Mahalia loved to skip along behind, clapping in time to the beat of the drum.

Now, in the 1920s, people could hear jazz on records. It was enjoyed in many homes, but Aunt Duke hated having it in her home. She thought only church music was good and proper and jazz was trash.

Mahalia and Peter had come to live with Aunt Duke and Uncle Emanuel when their mother died. Haley was only five years old at the time, and Peter ten. Their father, John Jackson, saw them often, but he could not stay at home to take care of them. Besides working on the docks during the day and cutting hair at a barbershop at night, he preached at the Baptist church on Sundays. Haley and Peter were happy in their new home. Even though Aunt Duke was strict, they felt sure of her love.

Mahalia glanced at the clock on the shelf. "Surely I can hear Bessie one more time before Aunt Duke gets home," she thought. She put on another record and sat down to sew on a scrap of cloth.

Just then, she heard the footsteps of a man bounding up onto the porch. "That's Fred," she thought, jumping up to greet him. The door burst open, and a tall,

handsome, smiling man came in. He scooped Mahalia up in his arms and swung her around.

"Ouch!" he cried. "Haley, you stabbed me!"

"Oh, I'm sorry, Cousin Fred. It was my needle. I'm making a doll," she explained.

"Honey, you never did have a real store-bought doll, did you?" Fred said, setting her down. "Someday I'm going to buy you one," he called over his shoulder as he went to hang up his coat.

Haley sat down again and, humming along with the record, made careful even stitches in the cloth. She wondered what Aunt Duke would bring home for supper. Aunt Duke worked as a cook for a rich white family. She was such a good cook that she earned ten dollars a week—a lot of money for a southern black woman in those days. Besides the ten dollars, she was given leftover food to bring home.

The front door opened suddenly, and Aunt Duke, dressed in a neat blue uniform, stepped inside. She was carrying a large pan, covered with a snowy white cloth. Haley leaped to her feet, her heart pounding.

"Mahalia Jackson!" Aunt Duke shouted.

"Are you playing those sinful jazz records?" The girl clutched her scrap of cloth and stood speechless. Aunt Duke put down the pan of food. She started for the corner where her whip was kept.

Fred came back into the room and quickly stepped between them. "No, Haley wasn't playing the records," he said, "*I* was." Fred bent over and covered his head with his arms. "Don't hit me! Please don't hit me!" he howled. Mahalia and Peter burst into laughter. The thought of Aunt Duke's raising a hand to her fun-loving only son was too much for them.

A half smile appeared on Aunt Duke's face, but she quickly put on her "stern look."

"Now put that record away, Fred," she said, "and Mahalia, you come and help

me in the kitchen." She moved briskly out of the room. Fred winked at Mahalia.

"Thanks," Haley whispered. She hurried into the kitchen and began to set the table before she was told. This was only one of Mahalia's chores. Since she was the only member of the family who didn't have a regular job, it was up to her to do all the work around the house before and after school. She also helped Uncle Emanuel weed the vegetable garden.

In the winter, Mahalia gathered firewood for the kitchen stove, and she picked up coal from along the railroad tracks for heat. Sometimes on Saturdays she and Peter would go to the swamps to look for turtles for soup, or they would catch fish in the Mississippi River. But most days Peter was busy doing yard work to earn money.

As Mahalia put the last of the plates on the table, Uncle Emanuel quietly came into the kitchen. "The table's all set, Haley? That's a good girl," he said, patting her on the shoulder. "I saw your daddy today," he went on, "and he said he's lonesome for you."

"I miss him, too. Maybe Peter and I can go to the barbershop to see him tonight." Turning to Aunt Duke, she asked, "Would it be all right?"

"Yes, after you've done your fifteen minutes of Bible reading. And, Mahalia, before I forget to tell you," she added, "you did a good job of scrubbing the kitchen this morning."

"Thank you, ma'am," Haley said, her face alight with a proud smile. To herself, she thought, "At least, I did *something* right today!"

16

2. A Sad Farewell

Mahalia folded the crisp white napkin she had just ironed and placed it on a large stack of finished laundry. "Only a few more pieces," she thought, glancing at the clock, "and then I can go home." It was nearly six o'clock, and she had been washing and ironing since early morning.

Mahalia had quit school after the eighth grade to go to work. She was only thirteen, but she had a grown-up job and she did it well. She could iron a man's shirt in just three minutes.

As she finished the last of the napkins, she sang "I'm So Glad Jesus Lifted Me Up." Her voice was strong and rich and sweet. It had an especially happy sound now, because Uncle Emanuel was coming home that night. He had been working in Chicago as a bricklayer, and Mahalia missed him very much. She was also

18

lonesome for Fred, who had gone to Kansas City to live. The house seemed empty without the two of them.

Mahalia put the ironing board away and hurried out the back door. She wanted to get home early enough to bake a sweet potato pie—her uncle's favorite—for supper. When she got there, Aunt Duke was already busy, and pots were bubbling on the stove. By the time Emanuel arrived, the kitchen was filled with tempting smells.

Mahalia hugged her uncle and quickly put the food on the table. "Come sit next to me, uncle," she called when the last steaming platter was in place.

Aunt Duke glanced sharply around the table to see that everything was in order. "You may say the blessing now, Mahalia," she said.

They all bowed their heads, and Mahalia repeated the familiar words: "Bless this house, oh, Lord, and we thank thee for this food."

Aunt Duke filled the plates and passed them around the table. Haley leaned close to her uncle. "Tell us about Chicago again," she begged. Emanuel smiled. He had told them about the northern city many times before, but Mahalia always wanted to hear more.

"It's a whole different kind of life there," Emanuel said. "Our people don't have to ride in the back of the bus like we do here in New Orleans. Up there we can even ride in taxis with white drivers. We can shop in white people's stores and try on clothes."

Mahalia was wide-eyed at the things Uncle Emanuel told them. She made a promise to herself. "I'll earn and save every penny I can," she thought. "And someday I'll go to Chicago, too."

The next day was Sunday, and Mahalia was up even earlier than usual. She loved any Sunday, for it meant going to church and singing, but today was a special day—Baptismal Sunday.

The family walked to church together. They arrived early and took their places on one of the wooden benches near the front. Mahalia sat quietly, her eyes on the door through which her father, the preacher, would come.

The little church filled quickly, and John Jackson entered to begin the service. After prayers and a sermon, he announced that it was time for the baptismal ceremony to begin. The women, all dressed in white, rose and led the way

out of the church. Singing "Let's Go Down to the River Jordan," they marched down the street to the nearby Mississippi River. The other people followed—all singing. Mahalia's clear, sweet voice soared over all the others.

At the river, she stood straight and proud as she watched her father lead prayers and bless the waters of the Mississippi. Then those children and adults who wanted to become members of the Baptist church stepped forward. One by one, Mr. Jackson led them into the river to be baptized. Mahalia remembered the day when she was lowered into the water. What a good feeling it had been to know that, from that moment on, she truly belonged to the Lord.

Before she went to bed that night, Mahalia said her prayers and thanked

God for a beautiful day. She thanked him for Uncle Emanuel's being home, too. "If only Fred were here," she thought, "then we'd be even happier." At last, smiling at memories of Fred's jokes and laughter, she drifted off to sleep.

In the middle of the night, she was awakened by the awful sounds of crying. She leaped from her bed and raced into the living room. Aunt Duke was pacing the floor, tears streaming down her face, her shoulders shaking with deep shuddering sobs. In her hand was a telegram.

Mahalia had never in her life seen Aunt Duke cry. The sight made her go cold with fear. "What is it? What's the matter?" she asked.

It took a moment for Aunt Duke to choke out an answer. "It's Fred," she moaned. "He's dead."

Haley stood frozen to the spot. "No!" she whispered. "It can't be true—not Fred." But it was true, and the family moved through the next few days numb with shock and sadness.

Fred's body was brought to New Orleans to be buried. At the funeral service in the Baptist church, Mahalia sat with lowered head and twisted a tear-soaked handkerchief. Afterwards, marching bands lined up in the street to lead the way to the cemetery on the edge of town. They marched slowly, in time to sad sounding music. Following were the hearse, the family, and a long line of Fred's friends.

After prayers at the cemetery, the bands began their march back to town. Now they played fast, lively music to show their joy that the dead person was in heaven. The followers behind the bands sang and clapped hands in time to the music.

Mahalia had often joined in the singing at other funerals. Now she wanted to sing for Fred. She wanted to be happy that he was in a place where nothing could ever hurt him, but how could she get over missing him? She opened her mouth, but try as she would, she could not make a sound. Her eyes blinded with tears, she could only plod along beside Aunt Duke. She clasped her hands tightly together and whispered, "Take good care of him, Lord."

3. A Dream Comes True

"You just forget about going to Chicago to live, Mahalia," Aunt Duke said. "You're going to stay right here where I can watch over you."

"But, Aunt Duke, I'm not a *child* anymore," Mahalia argued. "I'm *sixteen*." Big for her age, she was already taller and stronger than her aunt. She wore her hair piled high on her head in a style that made her look older than her years. But to Aunt Duke she was still a little girl.

"Chicago's a sinful city," Aunt Duke said, shaking a finger at Haley. "How do I know you wouldn't stop going to church?"

"I'd never do that," Mahalia answered. "I promise."

The argument went on for days, but at last Aunt Duke gave in. It was agreed that Mahalia would live in Chicago with her aunts, Hannah and Alice. Since Hannah was then visiting in New Orleans, she could take the girl back with her on the train.

On the morning Mahalia was to leave, a crowd of friends and relatives gathered at the station to say good-bye. In spite of Mahalia's joy in going "up North," she had to blink back tears as she hugged Aunt Duke, Uncle Emanuel, and her father.

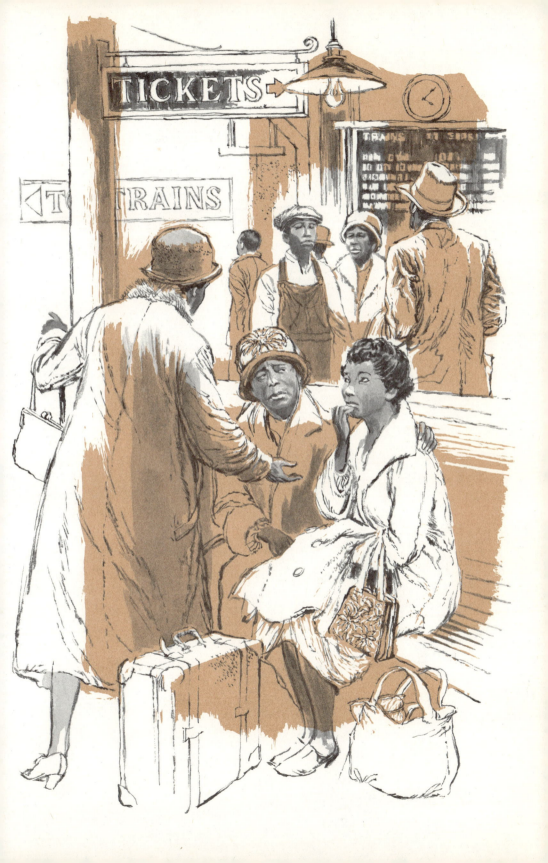

Aunt Duke said only, "You write, hear me?" But her eyes were wet. With one last backward look, Mahalia followed Aunt Hannah up the steps of the train.

It was a long trip to Chicago—two nights and a day—but Mahalia loved every minute of it.

In Chicago, they were greeted by icy December winds, and the streets were covered with snow. Mahalia was sure she had never been so cold.

Aunt Hannah hurried her into a taxi. When Mahalia saw that the driver was white, she thought, "It's really true what Uncle Emanuel told us. Here I am—in Chicago—riding in a white man's taxi."

Mahalia stared in amazement at the crowded, busy streets. She was used to the slow pace of New Orleans. Here, it seemed that everyone was in a hurry.

The rushing traffic frightened her, but it was exciting too.

She was soon settled with her aunts in a roomy, pleasant apartment. She found a job doing what she knew best—washing and ironing for several white families. She liked Chicago, but still she missed Aunt Duke and New Orleans. She also missed listening to her father's sermons in the friendly little Baptist church.

When her aunts took her to the Greater Salem Baptist Church, Mahalia was amazed. "I must write Aunt Duke about this," she thought. It was a big church, and there were 50 people in the choir. It seemed strange at first, but when the choir began to sing the songs Mahalia knew, she soon felt right at home. She sang and clapped hands and tapped her feet in time to the music, as everyone else did.

Before long, she met the preacher, the Reverend Johnson, and his family. When the Johnsons heard her sing, they asked her to be a member of the choir. Soon after, they asked her to sing solos. Mahalia was happy and proud to be a part of such a fine group. She went to choir practice several times a week and made many new friends. Though she still faithfully wrote Aunt Duke every week, she was over the ache of missing her.

One day, Mahalia read in the newspaper that Bessie Smith was going to perform in Chicago—the same Bessie she had heard on Cousin Fred's records.

"Aunt Alice, *please*, could we go hear Bessie Smith sing?" Mahalia's face showed how much she wanted this favor.

"I have enough money saved to buy tickets for both of us."

"I guess you do deserve a treat, Haley," Aunt Alice said. "You haven't done much in Chicago but work and go to church. All right, we'll go."

On the night of the performance, Mahalia hurried Aunt Alice so that they arrived at the theater much too early. When at last the show began, Mahalia, lost in the beautiful sounds of Bessie's songs, never moved in her seat. Even after the show was over, she sat gazing dreamily at the empty stage. Mahalia hoped she could hear Bessie again someday, but there was no extra money for theater tickets for a long time.

For suddenly, late in 1929, many American businesses failed. This was the start of the Great Depression. Millions

of people all over the country were soon
out of work. Money was scarce. Hungry
people lined up in "breadlines" and at
"soup kitchens," where they were given
a little free food.

Mahalia found it harder and harder to
get laundering jobs. Some weeks she

worked only two or three days. Usually she made only $1.75 a day. One day, as she was coming home from work in the growing darkness of late afternoon, Mahalia saw a small line of people. They were waiting to get their daily free loaf of bread.

She passed by the line, and then touched the crumpled dollar bill and the change in her coat pocket. She had washed clothes all day for that money, but she couldn't leave those tired looking, hopeless people behind her. She turned back and called, "You want a good meal? Follow me!"

Most of the people followed her. The rest, not trusting a stranger to feed a stranger, moved up in line for their loaves of bread. Mahalia and her followers' first stop was a grocery store. She bought a sack of potatoes and as much of the cheapest kind of meat as her money would buy.

She led her guests home, cooked the food, and served it. As soon as a plate was empty, she filled it again. At last no one could eat another bite. When the people had thanked her and said good-bye, Mahalia stood at the open door and smiled as she watched them walk away. She no longer felt tired from her day's work.

"The only trouble is," Mahalia thought, "I can't feed *everyone* who's hungry. But how I wish I could."

4. The Johnson Gospel Singers

One evening after choir practice, Mahalia stayed on in the church to talk to the three Johnson brothers and a girl named Louise Barry. One of the brothers, Prince, sat down at the piano and began to play a song they all knew. It was a gospel—a joyful song that praised the Lord. Mahalia began to sing, and the others joined in. The group sang well together, and soon they were all clapping hands in time to Prince's rhythm.

"Hey, that sounded great!" Robert Johnson said. "Why don't we pick out a

few more songs and practice them? We could sing at the church supper next week." They all agreed, and a new singing group was born—the Johnson Gospel Singers.

The Johnson Singers were a great success at the church supper. They were asked to sing again the next week. Soon people from other churches heard about the group and invited them to perform.

Tickets were sold to raise money for the churches, and each of the singers was paid—sometimes as much as $1.50 apiece. Mahalia wondered if she would ever be able to earn enough money singing to get away from the wash tubs.

"If I ever get any spare money," she thought, "I'll take singing lessons." It was 1932, and jobs were still hard to get. But Mahalia carefully saved nickels and dimes until she had enough to pay for one lesson. She coaxed her girl friend, also a singer, to go with her to a teacher named Professor DuBois.

"I'll hear you first, Miss Jackson," the professor said. He sat down at the piano and handed Mahalia a sheet of music. It was "Standing in the Need of Prayer," a song she knew well. As the professor played, she began to sing, softly at first. Then, before she knew it, she was singing louder and faster, giving a strong beat to the music.

"No! No!" the professor said, raising his hand to stop her. "Not like that. Now, listen to me." He sang a few lines slowly, as if the song were a funeral march. "Now try again," he said.

Mahalia tried, but it was no use. She could not hold back the joy and freedom

in her voice. The professor stopped her again.

He turned to Mahalia's friend. "Let's hear you sing it," he said. The girl sang the song slowly and softly as the teacher had.

"Fine. Fine." Professor DuBois nodded. "You may become a very good singer." To Mahalia, he said, "You don't sing. You *holler*! It will take a long time to teach you to sing."

The girls paid for their lesson and left. When they reached the street, Mahalia said, *"Four dollars* to have him tell me I *holler*. I'll never go back to him again." It was her first and last singing lesson.

There were plenty of other people who liked Mahalia's singing just as it was. The Johnson Gospel Singers were asked to appear at black churches outside of

Chicago. They sang in Saint Louis and Cleveland at the Baptist church conventions.

Mahalia enjoyed having an audience, and she loved to sing gospel. But not all the Johnson Singers felt as Mahalia did. Most of them found that all the traveling was too tiring, so Mahalia began to do some performances alone.

Once, when Mahalia came home from a long singing trip, she discovered she had lost her laundry jobs. She had been gone so long, other people had been hired in her place. For weeks, Mahalia searched for work. It was 1934, and the depression still dragged on. At last, she found a job as a maid, cleaning rooms in a hotel.

In the summer of that year, Mahalia's grandfather—her mother's father—came to Chicago to visit. Grandfather Paul had been born a slave on a cotton plantation in Louisiana. He loved to tell about life in the log cabin where his fifteen children were born. Mahalia adored him.

"Grandfather," she said one day, "it would be so nice for us if you would have your picture taken. Then we could always remember how you look."

"Who'd want a picture of an ugly old man like me?" he asked.

"All of us would like a picture, grandfather," Mahalia begged. "And I have some extra money to pay for it."

It took a lot of coaxing, but finally he gave in. One hot afternoon Mahalia and Aunt Hannah took him to the photographer's studio. There, as grandfather posed for his picture, a strange look suddenly came over his face. His eyes closed, and he slumped to the floor.

"Papa! What's the matter?" Aunt Hannah cried. The old man lay motionless. They managed to get him into a taxi and rushed to the hospital.

Mahalia sat on a bench in the hospital hall near the door to grandfather's room. Aunt Hannah, beside her, was dabbing at her eyes with her handkerchief. When the doctor came out of the room, Hannah said, "How is he, doctor? Is he going to be all right?"

"He's a very sick man," the doctor said. "You'd better stay here through the night."

Aunt Hannah was wild with worry. Tears were pouring down her cheeks. "It's your fault, Haley!" she cried. "Papa never should have gone out in this awful heat, and you made him do it!"

Mahalia felt as though she had been

struck. Surely she loved grandfather as much as anyone. She got to her feet and stumbled down the hall to an empty room. She knelt down to pray. "Please, God," she said, "I'm sorry if I did anything wrong. Please let grandfather live. I'll do anything if you will—anything."

She would make a bargain with God. She began to think of what she could give him in trade for her grandfather's life. It must be something she really loved. "I know," she thought. "The theater—the movies—stage shows—Bessie Smith."

"Dear God," she prayed, "make my grandfather well, and I'll never go into a movie theater again." Haley repeated the prayer over and over for nine days. At last the old man got well, and she fell on her knees once more to thank God for answering her prayers.

"Thank you, Lord," she said. "I'll keep my promise."

5. "I Sing for the Lord"

Mahalia filled her cup with coffee and turned to find a place to sit. The church basement was crowded with people who had come to hear the Johnson Gospel Singers.

"Won't you sit here, Miss Jackson?" a man's voice asked. She looked into the face of a stranger who was standing beside her. The man waved a hand toward two chairs.

Mahalia's warm, lovely smile lit her face. She nodded and sat down. "You know my name," she said, "but I don't know yours."

"I'm Isaac Hockenhull," he said, "but my friends call me Ike."

"Well, my friends call me Haley, and we're all friends in the Greater Salem Baptist Church."

They talked easily together. Mahalia learned that Ike was 34, ten years older than she was. He was a college graduate, and she was a little surprised that he was interested in her.

Ike walked home with Mahalia that night and many nights afterwards. Before long they knew they were in love and wanted to marry. Ike had studied to be a chemist, but the only work he could find now was that of a postman. In 1936 postmen were paid very little money, and Mahalia was not earning much either. They decided to get married anyway and to live with Aunt Hannah until they could afford their own place. About a year after their marriage, they were able to rent a small apartment.

Although Ike was proud of Mahalia's voice, he was always unhappy when she went away on singing trips. Every time he saw her packing a suitcase, an argument would begin.

"Haley, when are you going to stop this gospel singing? You should be studying to be a concert singer. You're wasting your voice on something that isn't even good music!"

"The Lord gave me this voice," Mahalia would say, "and I want to use it to praise him. The Bible says, 'Make a joyful noise unto the Lord,' and that's what makes me happy." She would not give in, and Ike would not stop nagging her about it.

Once, she came back after a singing trip and found she had lost her job as a hotel maid. This was a bad time, because Ike was out of work, too.

"Look at this, Haley," Ike said, handing her a newspaper clipping. "They're looking for a woman to play one of the leading parts in a black jazz show—*The Hot Mikado*. You should try out for it."

Mahalia barely glanced at the clipping. "You know I don't want to sing that kind of music," she said.

"Listen, Haley, we've been living on red beans and rice for a week. What's more, the rent has to be paid. I'm going to look for work, and you'd better do the same." Ike left, and Mahalia sat staring sadly at the clipping.

At last, she made herself go to the theater where the tryouts were being held. Mahalia was shown to a seat, where she was to wait her turn to sing. A dozen or more girls who were there ahead of her whispered excitedly as they watched the singer on stage.

Mahalia felt more and more unhappy. "I promised God I wouldn't go to the theater," she thought. "And I never have. It doesn't seem right to sing in one either."

When her name was finally called, Mahalia moved with dragging steps to the stage. She sang "Sometimes I Feel like a Motherless Child." The sad song matched her feelings exactly. There was instant silence in the theater as her voice poured forth, as smooth and rich as cream. The men who were hiring the singers sat forward in their seats as they watched her.

When she was finished, Mahalia saw the men whispering together. She had a feeling that she was going to get the job whether she wanted it or not. She left as the next singer took her place.

When she got home Ike was waiting for her. "Haley!" he shouted, hugging her. "You got the part. They just called from the theater. I'm so proud of you."

"Thank you, Ike," Mahalia said sadly.

"And I got a job, too," Ike said.

"You *did*? You really did?" Mahalia's voice brightened. "Then I don't have to sing jazz. I'm not going to be in that show."

Ike couldn't believe she would pass up her big chance. He argued and pleaded with her, but nothing would make her change her mind. The only thing Mahalia wanted to do was to "sing for the Lord."

6. "Movin' On Up"

In 1937 Decca Records asked Mahalia to make her first record. It was a song popular in the South, "God Gonna Separate the Wheat from the Tares." Because few people understood the title, the record was only mildly successful; but Mahalia was glad to have made a start in recording.

Even without a hit record, she was able to stop working as a hotel maid. The depression was almost over, and she was earning more and more money singing at black gospel meetings all over the country.

Still Mahalia didn't feel safe from hard times. "If another depression comes," Mahalia thought, "I'm going to be ready for it. I want to have my own business."

In her spare time, she took lessons in hairdressing, and she carefully saved money from her singing. By 1939 she was able to open a beauty shop. Most of the women who belonged to her church became her customers. Soon she had to hire five girls to work in the shop. Now she was able to send money to her family.

Mahalia did not feel safe yet. She began to study flower arranging, and before long she opened a florist shop. This business was a success too.

Mahalia was glad she had her shops and her music to keep her busy. She

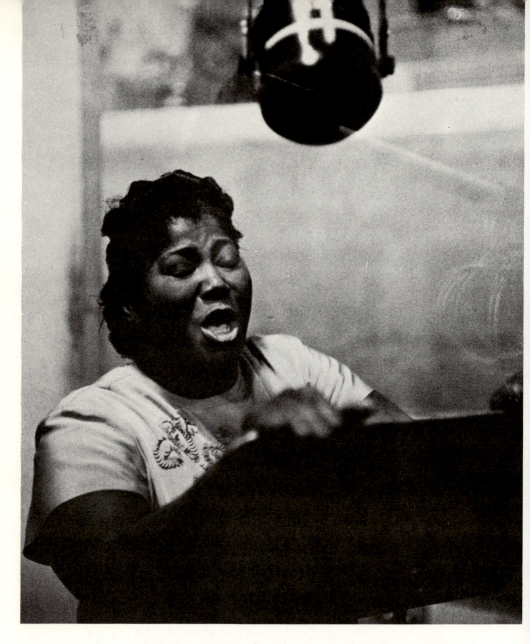

Mahalia expressed in gospel song her love of God and her deep and abiding faith. This photograph was taken at one of her early recording sessions.

was living alone now, for she and Ike had parted. They were still good friends, but both of them knew they would never agree on her gospel singing.

Gospel was becoming more popular, and Mahalia was recording often, but it was not until 1946 that she had a real hit record. It happened almost by accident. Mahalia was in the Apollo Records studio waiting for the engineers to set up their equipment. To warm up her voice, she sang a song she had known as a child in New Orleans.

"Mahalia, what is that you're singing?" asked Bess Burma, who worked for the recording company.

"Oh, it's just an old southern song we used to call 'Movin' On Up.' "

"I've never heard it before, and you sing it beautifully," Bess said. "Let's record it." They did, and "I Will Move On Up a Little Higher" was a huge success.

Now Mahalia decided she could afford to hire her own piano player to accompany her when she sang. She chose Mildred Falls, a talented, soft-spoken woman. The two women practiced together, traveled together, and during all the years they worked together, remained close friends.

One day in 1950 as they were practicing, a white music teacher from New York called to ask Mahalia to come to Music Inn in Massachusetts for a week. He wanted her to sing for a group of teachers who were studying the beginnings of American folk music. It was the first time Mahalia had been asked to sing for an all-white audience.

60

"I can't think what those music teachers want of me," she said to Mildred, "but let's find out." They arrived at Music Inn just before the evening meal. Afterwards, everyone gathered in a big room where there was a piano. Mahalia faced her audience and began to sing.

She seemed to be singing directly to the Lord. Her voice praised God with deep love and warmth and joy. The people listening felt caught up in her great outpouring of faith.

"Where did you learn to sing like that?" one of the teachers asked when the song was finished. "Who taught you?"

"No one taught me," Mahalia said. "I just sing the way I feel."

There were more questions. "What is gospel?" "Where did it come from?"

"From my people," she told them. "To make their life a little more bearable when they were slaves, they sang as they worked in the fields. The songs they made up, called 'spirituals,' were sad songs, but they told of a better life in heaven.

"When they were freed from slavery," she went on, "their songs were happy ones. They were sure that life was going to get better for them. These songs were called 'jubilees,' and gospel has some of both spirituals and jubilees in it."

"Won't you sing another song?" the teachers urged. They kept her singing for hours. At the end of the week, one of the men stopped her to tell her how they felt about her singing.

"Miss Jackson," he said, "if you had walked down to the lake while you were singing 'Shall We Gather at the River,' everyone would have followed you into the water to be baptized."

The teachers at Music Inn told all the important people in the music world about Mahalia. Once back in Chicago, she received many requests to perform. She appeared on a coast-to-coast television show. Then came a chance to do a

Mahalia charmed the audience at Music Inn with her moving rendition of gospel songs.

concert at New York's Carnegie Hall—
one of the greatest of honors for any
performer. Mahalia was not yet 40, and
she was at last really "movin' on up."

On the night of the concert, when
Mahalia walked onto the stage, she
caught her breath in surprise. Every seat
in the huge hall was filled, and more
people were sitting on folding chairs
around the edge of the stage. There was
only a small space beside the piano for
Mahalia to stand.

"All of these people are here to see
me?" she thought. She was afraid she
would not be able to sing a note, but
Mildred was already playing the opening
bars of her first song. Mahalia clasped
her hands together and closed her eyes.
Gathering courage, she lifted her head
and began to sing "Oh, Lamb of God."

As her singing became more and more joyous, the audience clapped and stomped in time to the music. Many had tears streaming down their faces. When Mahalia finished and left the stage, the entire audience stood to clap and cheer. They shouted for her to come back time and time again.

When it was all over, Mahalia sank wearily into a chair backstage. "Just think, Mildred," she said, "*me*—a black washerwoman from the South—singing in Carnegie Hall."

"Black washerwoman or not, Mahalia, they loved you," Mildred said.

People in other countries loved Mahalia's voice, too. In 1952 her recording of "I Can Put My Trust in Jesus" was given a prize by the French Academy of Music. She felt she owed it to the

Mahalia accepts an armload of tulips in Holland and (right) sings that evening for an enthusiastic Dutch audience.

people of France to thank them in person, so she planned a tour of Europe.

When she and Mildred arrived in Paris, they were met by a great crowd of people. Policemen had to hold back the excited fans to keep Mahalia from being trampled. The concert hall where she sang that night was completely filled.

She went on to sing in Holland, then Denmark and Belgium. Most of the people didn't know English well enough to understand all the words at her performances, but they could understand the love of God which she put in her songs.

Again and again, her audiences clapped and begged for "just one more song." Mahalia couldn't say no, but after that song, they always asked for "just one more."

"You're wearing yourself out, Mahalia,"

Mildred warned her. "You must think of yourself. You're working too hard."

Mahalia knew Mildred was right, but she said, "Singing for the Lord isn't work. It's what I was born to do."

Suddenly one night, Mahalia fainted on the stage. Doctors were called, and she was taken to a hospital. After a few days, she was strong enough to be helped onto a plane to go home. Mahalia was afraid of flying, but this time she was too ill to argue. She was more tired than she had ever been before.

Settled comfortably in bed in a Chicago hospital, Mahalia began to feel better. "Weren't all those people lovely to me?" she thought. "I'll go back there again some day when I'm well again." She turned her head on the pillow and fell into a deep, restful sleep.

7. Mahalia Finds a New Home

After her stay in the hospital, Mahalia rested for a long time. By the spring of 1954, she was ready and anxious to sing again. She had earned enough money to be able to live without working for the rest of her life. She also knew that she must not become overtired by too much traveling, but she missed the excitement of performing.

When an offer came for her to do a weekly radio show for CBS in Chicago, she accepted at once. She could work without even leaving her home town.

Mahalia appeared on radio and television with stars of the entertainment world. She is seen here with Duke Ellington.

Later her show was switched from radio to television. The director asked Mahalia to learn some Irish and Jewish and popular songs.

Mahalia had to work hard to prepare new songs for the show each week. She could not read a note of music. Mildred would play a song over and over while Mahalia read the words and learned the tune by heart. They often practiced in Mahalia's apartment, and sometimes they could be heard far into the night. Time after time other people in the six-story building knocked on her door to complain that her singing disturbed them.

"What I need is a house of my own," Mahalia thought, "with nobody living above or below me."

She began to look for a new home. In Chicago, as in most American towns and cities at that time, few white people would sell their houses to blacks. Few black people had fine houses to sell. Finally Mahalia found a white couple who agreed to sell her their house.

The people in the area were very angry when they heard that a black woman wanted to move into their neighborhood. Mahalia began to get phone calls which warned her, "Move in there and we'll blow up the house." Mahalia was sick at heart.

She prayed to God to help her decide what to do. She could not believe she was doing anything wrong. Finally, she bought the house and moved in.

A few nights later, some of the windows were shot out. Mahalia called friends, who came and stayed with her for weeks. When the windows were shot at again, she asked the police for help. For almost a year, they guarded her house.

When Mahalia at last felt safe, she began to enjoy her new home. She loved to cook, and nothing pleased her more than preparing dinner for a big group of friends. Best of all, she could sing whenever she liked. She sang for her many friends and relatives when they visited, and she and Mildred practiced and practiced.

Shortly after Mahalia got her house, she went to Denver, Colorado, to sing at the National Baptist Convention. There she met two young black ministers from Montgomery, Alabama. One was the Reverend Ralph D. Abernathy, and the other was Dr. Martin Luther King, Jr.

They told Mahalia about what was happening in their city. Black people were no longer willing to ride in the back of the buses and give up their seats to white people. They had agreed not to use the buses at all until they were allowed to sit any place they liked.

"Now we're trying to get cars to help our people get to and from work," Dr. King said. "Miss Jackson, could we hire you to sing in Montgomery to help raise the money?"

"Of course, I'll come," Mahalia said, "and I'll sing for nothing." She thought of the months when she needed police protection in her own home. It was time blacks worked together for their rights. She kept her promise and went to Montgomery to sing. While there she was welcomed into the King and Abernathy homes and became a close friend of both families.

Martin Luther King inspired Mahalia to devote her talents to the civil rights movement.

Dr. King began traveling throughout the South to try to gain equal rights for black people. The southern whites did everything they could to stop him. In 1960 he was arrested in Atlanta, Georgia, and the judge ordered him to spend four months in jail. Blacks all over the country were angry at the news.

John F. Kennedy was then running for the presidency, and he helped to get Dr.

King out of jail. When election day arrived, millions of black Americans turned out to vote for Kennedy. Mahalia was among them, and she was thrilled when Kennedy won.

Soon afterwards, Mahalia called Mildred to ask, "How would you like to go to a party—a very special party?"

"Whose party? Where?" Mildred asked.

"A party in Washington for John F. Kennedy! Can you believe it? They asked me to sing 'The Star-Spangled Banner.'" The words came tumbling over each other. "It will be on the night before he takes office as president."

"Wonderful!" Mildred said. "But you've never sung that song in public before. We'd better start practicing right now."

The mayor of Chicago, Richard Daley, invited them to ride to Washington with him in a special railroad car. As the train rolled along, Mahalia thought of her first train ride, when she came to Chicago as a wide-eyed girl of sixteen. Now she was riding with the mayor of Chicago, and she was going to sing for the president of the United States!

Mildred and Mahalia arrived at the party dressed in new long dresses bought especially for the great event. When they walked through the crowd in the huge hall, Mahalia whispered, "Did you ever see so many famous people gathered in one room?" There were actors and actresses, singers, dancers, bandleaders. It seemed that everyone important in the entertainment world was there.

By the time Mahalia was to sing, she was tingling with excitement. The lights were dimmed, and she stood alone on the

stage in the glow of a spotlight. She
sang the song as perfectly as if she had
written the words herself. The crowd
stood in utter silence until the last note
faded away. Then the audience burst into
applause. Mahalia felt tears come to her
eyes as she stepped down from the stage.

When the long program ended, Mahalia
looked up from her table to see John
Kennedy coming toward her. "I enjoyed
your singing very much, Miss Jackson,"
he said, shaking her hand. "Thank you
for coming."

"I'm so glad you liked it," Mahalia
said. As he moved on to greet the other
performers, she said to Mildred, "That
was kind and thoughtful of him. No
wonder people like him so much. I'll remember this night for the rest of my
life."

8. To the Holy Land

Since childhood, Mahalia had longed to visit the places where Jesus was born, lived, and died. She had read about them in her daily Bible-reading—and sung about them in her concerts. Now she decided it was time to see them for herself.

"I'm almost 50 years old," she thought, "and if I wait too long I may never get there." She began to make plans. She would do another concert tour of Europe with a side trip to the Holy Land. The tour was soon arranged, and Mahalia

and Mildred sailed for their first stop, England.

Their London concert was held at the Royal Albert Hall. Mahalia's audience completely filled the huge building.

Afterwards, as Mahalia and Mildred were leaving, they were amazed to find a mob of people waiting by the stage door for autographs. The crowd pushed forward so eagerly that Mahalia was knocked down. She had to crawl on her hands and knees to reach her waiting car.

"Lord, give me the strength to last through this tour," she prayed.

Mahalia sang in Germany, then in Denmark, Sweden, Holland, and France in about a month's time. Once more, Mildred warned her she was wearing herself out.

"I know, I know," Mahalia said, "but

soon we'll go to the Holy Land, and I'll have my reward."

They made the trip by train, then by boat, and finally in a car with an Arab driver. It was a tiring journey, but Mahalia became more and more excited as they drew nearer her goal. When they reached the River Jordan, Mahalia said to the driver, "Stop the car. I want to get out for a minute." She knelt beside the river and let the holy water run through her hands. She thanked God for seeing her safely there.

They went on to Bethlehem where Christ was born, and at last to Jerusalem. There, in a church on the spot where it is believed Jesus was nailed to the cross, Mahalia knelt again. She remembered Christ's suffering here. Tears rolled down her cheeks as she prayed.

"Now we can go home," she said to Mildred. "I've seen what I came to see— all of the places I've been singing about for so long." On the ship going home, Mahalia spent most of her time resting in her room. She thought she had never been so tired.

Soon after she returned to Chicago, she and Mildred started off on a nationwide tour of "one-night stands." They would perform in a different town every night, driving miles and miles by day. Finally, Mahalia no longer had the strength to go on. Her manager took her back to Chicago to a hospital.

The doctors said her heart was weak. She had strained it by working too hard for so many years. "You need a *long* rest, Miss Jackson," the doctors told her. Mahalia had to agree.

By 1963 her health was much better, and she was anxious to sing again. She was happy when Martin Luther King, Jr., called her to ask if she would come to Washington to take part in an important program. He explained that both blacks and whites from all over the country were going to march in the city. They

Dr. Martin Luther King leads the historic March on Washington, August 28, 1963.

wanted to show the government how many people were banding together to work for equal rights for blacks.

"Of course I'll be there," Mahalia said.

Mahalia and Mildred drove 680 miles to Washington the night before the march was to take place. All during the night and the next morning, people poured into the city. They came by bus, train, plane, and even on foot. At noon, Dr. King led the 200,000 marchers through the streets to the Lincoln Memorial.

Chairs had been placed in front of the big statue of Abraham Lincoln, and Mahalia was seated in one near Dr. King. On one side of the platform was a piano for Mildred.

When it was time for her to sing, Mahalia rose and went to the microphone. She looked out over a sea of faces

that stretched farther than her eyes
could see. Softly Mahalia began to sing:

I been 'buked and I been scorned.
I'm gonna tell my Lord
When I get home
Just how long
  you've been treating me wrong.

Then her joy in seeing this great
crowd began to show in her voice. She
quickened the beat and clapped her
hands. Thousands of hands clapped with
her.

Afterwards, Martin Luther King gave
one of his finest speeches. It began, "I
have a dream," and it told of his hopes
for blacks and whites living as equals.

As Mahalia listened, she thought, "At
last my people have a leader who will

help them find the way to freedom." She went home happy and proud that she had been asked to take part in the day's events.

Her happiness lasted only a few months, however, for on November 22, 1963, a tragedy stunned the entire nation. President Kennedy was killed in Dallas, Texas. Mahalia wept for the loss of such a fine young man.

"I feel like I've lost a dear, close friend," she said to Mildred. "In fact, every black person in America has lost a friend."

9. A Great Voice Is Stilled

Kennedy's sad death filled Mahalia's thoughts for months. One of the people who tried to cheer her up was an old friend, Sigmund Galloway. He was a tall, handsome man, who shared her love of music. He played popular music in an orchestra, but he liked gospel music too.

Mahalia had many friends, but she began to realize that for a long time she had been lonely. She had divorced Ike many years ago, and most of her family was in the South. She enjoyed going to dinners and parties with Sigmund. When he asked her to marry him, she accepted. They were married in 1965.

Mahalia continued to sing, and she gave more and more of her time to helping Martin Luther King in his work. In 1966 she appeared with him at Soldiers' Field in Chicago before an audience of over 50,000 people. At another King meeting, she not only sang but also paid the rent for the building where he spoke.

The songs people most liked to hear at these meetings were called Freedom Songs. Many of them were the spirituals that slaves had sung as they hoped and prayed for a better life. Some had new words set to the music of old hymns. The most popular song of all was "We

Shall Overcome." Mahalia sang it at meetings time after time.

We shall overcome, we shall overcome,
We shall overcome some day.
Oh, deep in my heart I do believe
We shall overcome some day.©

Mahalia recorded the song in an album called "Mahalia Jackson Sings the Best-Loved Hymns of Dr. Martin Luther King, Jr."

Then, in April of 1968, Mahalia was again crushed by sorrow. Martin Luther King was shot and killed in Memphis, Tennessee. This was a blow that seemed almost too much for her to bear. She was asked to sing at the funeral in Atlanta, Georgia. Sadly, she agreed to do so.

At the funeral of Dr. Martin Luther King,
Mahalia sings for her lost friend.

To Mildred, she said, "I don't know if I can do it. It will be the hardest thing I'll ever have to do in my whole life."

Mahalia sang "Precious Lord, Take My Hand" and sang it beautifully. Her eyes were wet with tears, and a hushed crowd wept with her. Television cameras filmed the funeral, and Mahalia's song expressed the great sense of loss felt by all the people watching at home.

Mahalia went back to Chicago with a heavy heart. As always when she was troubled, she tried to keep busy with her singing. There were more concerts, more television appearances, more recording sessions. The money she earned was not important to her. She gave much of it to help good causes or to friends and relatives who needed it.

But her work did not seem to give her

the joy it once had. Her marriage to Sigmund was not a happy one, and they were divorced. Brother Peter was dead; Aunt Duke was dead; and Mahalia felt tired and alone.

Early in 1972, her doctor ordered her into the hospital for an operation. After the surgery was over, her great warm heart gave up under the strain of years. Sixty-year-old Mahalia died on January 27.

When she was buried just outside New Orleans, a message from the president was read. It told how people the world over felt about Mahalia Jackson. "Millions of ears will miss the sound of that great, rich voice making a joyful noise unto the Lord."

Index